Spotlight on Reading

Compare and Contrast
Grades 3–4

Frank Schaffer

An imprint of Carson-Dellosa Publishing LLC
Greensboro, North Carolina

Credits

Layout and Cover Design: Van Harris
Development House: The Research Masters

Cover Photo: © Getty Images

This book has been correlated to state, common core state, national, and Canadian provincial standards. Visit *www.carsondellosa.com* to search for and view its correlations to your standards.

Frank Schaffer
An imprint of Carson-Dellosa Publishing LLC
PO Box 35665
Greensboro, NC 27425 USA
www.carsondellosa.com

About the Book

The activities in *Compare and Contrast* are designed to improve students' reading comprehension skills and to give them the skills necessary for finding similarities and differences in text. With a variety of fun and instructional formats, teachers can provide an introduction, reinforcement, or independent practice for this essential reading skill. To ensure a high level of interest, a variety of activities and topics are included in this workbook.

Use these selections for independent practice or whole-group instruction. Have students work with partners or teams to complete the more challenging activities. Another idea is to place the activity sheets in a center and reproduce the answer key for self-checking.

• •

Table of Contents

Name _____

What Is for Breakfast?

Look at the pictures of the two breakfast cereals. Answer the questions that follow.

• •

a. Nature Grain Cereal   b. Sugar-Coated Cookie Cereal

_____ 1. Which cereal has oat bran in it?

_____ 2. Which cereal has the higher sugar content?

_____ 3. Which cereal has the lower protein content?

_____ 4. Which cereal contains raisins?

_____ 5. Which cereal contains chocolate chip cookies?

_____ 6. Keesha loves to exercise and eat healthy foods. Which cereal would she eat for breakfast?

_____ 7. Gary has a sweet tooth. Which cereal would he ask his mother to buy at the store?

Try this: On a separate piece of paper write another name for each cereal.

Name _____

A Dog's Life

Read the descriptions of the two dogs. Answer the questions that follow.

George lives with his family in the country. He has lots of room to run and play. His favorite toy is a tennis ball. When his owner is not home, he likes to lay around and chew on rawhide bones.

Princess lives in the city with her family. She has her own key so she can go for a walk in the park. Her favorite toy is a plastic pink ball. After Princess's humans leave for work, she likes to have the other dogs in the neighborhood over for tea.

1. What kind of toy do both dogs like? _____

2. Which dog can play ball in its own yard? _____

3. Which dog plays in the park? _____

4. Which dog probably spends more time outside than inside? _____

    _____

5. Which dog description is fiction (not real)? _____

    Write a sentence explaining how you know one of the descriptions is fiction.

    _____

    _____

Try this: Read the nonfiction description again. What clues show it is nonfiction (real)? List them on a separate piece of paper.

Five-Day Forecast

Look at the following five-day forecast. Answer the questions that follow.

1. Sue is planning a picnic this week. She wants it to be sunny and hot so Sue and her friends can picnic in the shade. What day would be the best for her picnic? _____

2. Ken is going fishing with a friend. He likes to fish when it is cloudy but not raining. Which day would be the best for him to go fishing? _____
   _____

3. Steve's baseball team is playing its first game on Monday. Does it look like the game will be rained out? _____

4. Tammy plans to see a movie on a day when it is likely to rain. Which day should she choose? _____

5. Jason and Tyler want to go to the beach on the warmest day this week. Which day should they choose? _____

6. Jean just got a new sweater. Which day might be the best day to wear it? _____

Name _____

Read each pair of statements below. If the statement is an example of nonfiction, write **NF** on the line next to it. If the statement is an example of fiction, write an **F** on the line next to it.

_____ 1. a. Turtles have hard shells.

_____   b. Turtles use their hard shells to play hide and seek.

_____ 2. a. The elf made a dress out of leaves.

_____   b. Leaves come in many shapes, sizes, and colors.

_____ 3. a. The thermometer showed the temperature was below freezing.

_____   b. The thermometer put on a coat to keep warm in the freezing cold.

_____ 4. a. Ladybugs have wings.

_____   b. Ladybugs are grouchy.

_____ 5. a. Cows can jump over the moon.

_____   b. Milk comes from cows.

_____ 6. a. Baseball is played with a bat and a ball.

_____   b. The bat told the baseball, "You are going on a flight!"

_____ 7. a. The mice in the attic sewed a ball dress.

_____   b. Mice live in the attics of some homes.

Try this: On a separate piece of paper write a sentence and have a friend tell you if it is fiction or nonfiction.

Name _____

Read each pair of words. Circle the word that belongs in the blank.

• •

1. Nap is to sleep as _____ is to mail.

            motor   letter   nurse

2. Dim is to bright as weak is to _____ .

            strong   loose   dangerous

3. Creek is to brook as _____ is to path.

            trail   garden   house

4. Rabbit is to bunny as _____ is to calf.

            horse   bird   cow

5. Slick is to slippery as _____ is to fast.

            swift   slow   old

6. Bed is to boy as _____ is to baby.

            feather   dentist   crib

7. Steel is to car as _____ is to house.

            brass   wood   silver

8. Poodle is to dog as _____ is to bird.

            lion   spider   sparrow

9. Niece is to nephew as sister is to _____ .

            aunt   father   brother

Try this: How are the words **old** and **new** related? On a separate piece of paper write three more pairs of words that are related in the same way.

Name _____

Animal Diagram

Review the Venn diagram. Answer the questions below.

Circle 1

spotted skunk

lady bug

Dalmatian

cheetah

leopard

Circle 2

lion

panther

tiger

1. What is true of all the things in Circle 1, including where the circles overlap? _____

   _____

2. What is true of all the things in Circle 2, including where the circles overlap? _____

   _____

3. What would be a good title for this diagram? _____

   _____

4. How would you label each section of the diagram?

   Circle 1: _____

   Circle 2: _____

Name _____

Read the facts about the North and South Poles. Underline the facts which are true about the South Pole in red. Underline the facts which are true about the North Pole in blue.

· ·

The Earth acts like a giant magnet. It has two poles just like a magnet. They are called the North and the South Poles. These poles are magnet poles, not tall metal or wooden poles.

The area called the North Pole is floating ice, not land. This huge ice pack floats on the Arctic Ocean. The North Pole is very cold. In 1909, Robert E. Peary traveled by dogsled to the North Pole. He was the first known human to arrive there. In 1958, a submarine, the USS Nautilus, traveled under this pole. This proved that the pole really was made of floating ice.

The South Pole is land covered by ice and snow. It is on the continent of Antarctica. This pole is the coldest and driest place on Earth. The temperature never gets warm enough to melt the ice and snow. There is a blanket of ice two miles (three kilometers) thick over the pole.

The first known person to reach this pole was Roald Amundsen in 1911. He also used dogsleds—his were pulled by 52 dogs. The 1,860-mile (2993 kilometer) trip took 99 days.

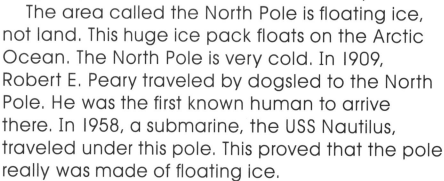

Name _____

Study the facts you have collected about the poles. Complete the Venn diagram below.

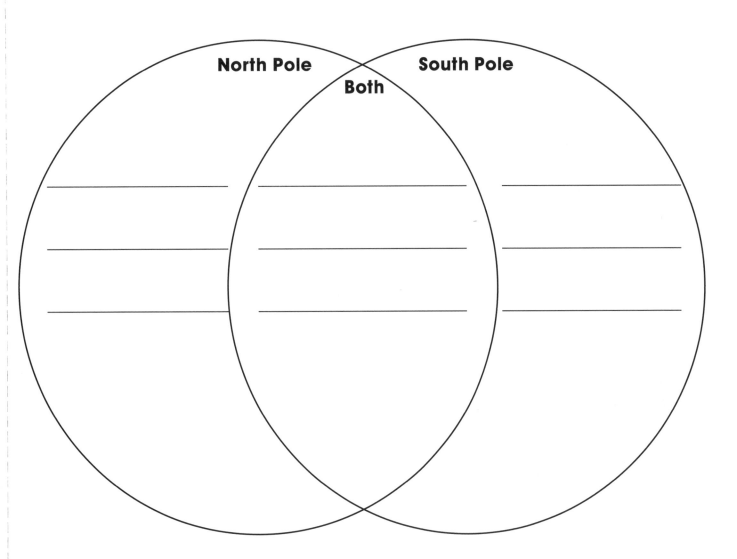

North Pole　　**Both**　　**South Pole**

- -

Try This: Would you like to go to the North or South Pole? On a separate piece of paper write why or why not.

- -

All Packed Up

Look at the different contents of the backpacks. Answer the questions below.

1. Who plays an instrument? _____

2. Who has gym class today? _____

3. Who brought fruit for snack? _____

4. Who is going to a birthday party after school? _____

5. Who brought a note to his or her teacher from home? _____

6. Who has new pencils to use today? _____

7. Who is buying lunch today at the cafeteria? _____

8. Who will not be returning a book at the library today? _____

Try this: Choose a backpack above. On a separate piece of
paper write a story about a day at school and mention each
item in the pack as a part of the story.

Word Sorts

Compare the words in the Word Bank. Sort them into the categories by writing each word under the correct title in the table.

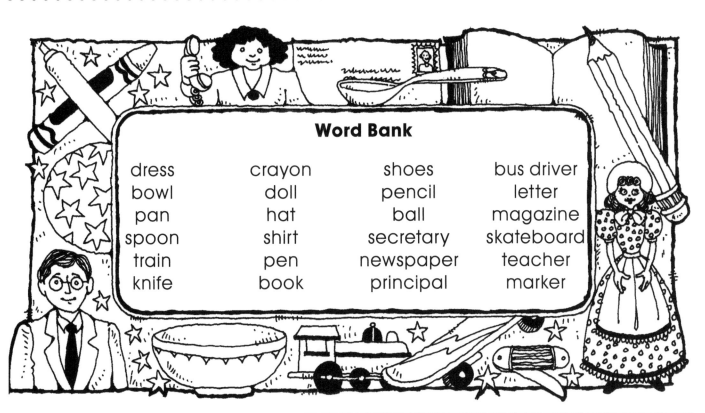

Word Bank

dress	crayon	shoes	bus driver
bowl	doll	pencil	letter
pan	hat	ball	magazine
spoon	shirt	secretary	skateboard
train	pen	newspaper	teacher
knife	book	principal	marker

Clothing	School Workers	Toys

Things to Read	Writing Tools	Kitchen Tools

Name _____

Similes Are Like . . .

Complete the following similes by matching the first part of the sentence to a phrase that makes sense. Draw a line from column one to its best match in column two. Then use the Word Bank to fill in both parts of the similes below.

Column One

1. The bride's dress was as white as
2. The mountain was as high as
3. The diamond sparkled like
4. The angry dog growled like
5. The stale bread was as hard as
6. The athlete ran like

Column Two

a. a star.
b. a rock.
c. the moon.
d. a deer.
e. a bear.
f. snow.

Word Bank

clown   clay   ice   hyena   dough   popsicle

7. The _____ was as cold as _____ .

8. The _____ felt like _____ .

9. The _____ laughed like a _____ .

Compare and Contrast • CD-104540

Best Friends

Read the following description of Jeff and Derek. Answer the questions below by circling Yes or No or writing words.

• •

Jeff and Derek are best friends. They are in the same class at school, and they are on the same soccer team. Jeff is eight years old, and Derek is nine years old. Derek rides a bus to school, but Jeff walks. Jeff loves to play outside, but Derek would rather play indoor games. In school, Jeff is very good at math. Derek is a good writer. They both love recess time!

1. Both Jeff and Derek play soccer.   Yes   No
2. Both Jeff and Derek are the same age.   Yes   No
3. Both Jeff and Derek like to play outside.   Yes   No
4. Jeff likes math more than Derek does.   Yes   No
5. Both Jeff and Derek dislike recess.   Yes   No

6. When the boys are together, who might want to ride bikes?

    _____

7. Who would rather play a video game? _____

8. Who would be good at writing a letter to a friend who has moved away?

    _____

9. At the candy store, who would be best at figuring out how much they can buy with their money?_____

> **Try this:** On a separate piece of paper make a list of the ways that you and a friend are the same and different.

Football and Soccer

Read the passage comparing football and soccer. Answer the questions on the next page.

• •

Football is played mainly in the United States and Canada. It is played with an oval ball. The field is about 120 yards (110 meters) long and 54 yards (49 meters) wide. It is played with two teams of 11 players each. The players must wear protective gear. The game starts with a kickoff. Players run or pass the ball as they try to score a touchdown. A touchdown gives the team six points.

Soccer is played all over the world. It is played with a round ball. The size of a soccer field. It may be 100–130 yards long (91–119 meters) and 50–100 yards wide (46–91 meters). It is played with two teams of 11 players each. Players also wear protective gear. The game starts with a kickoff. Players kick or head the ball to try to score a goal. A goal in soccer is worth one point.

Football and Soccer (cont.)

Fill in the Venn diagram to show the similarities and differences between football and soccer.

• •

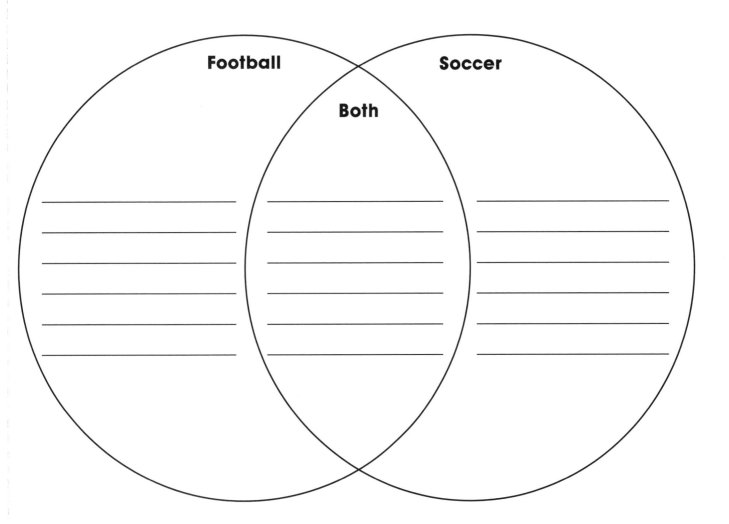

Football   **Soccer**

Both

Name _____

Hurricanes and tornadoes are both powerful storms. People often confuse the two. Read the passage to learn facts about the storms. Answer the questions about the similarities and differences.

• •

Hurricanes are powerful storms. They develop over warm ocean water. In the U.S. the hurricane season is from June to November. Winds move more than 75 miles (120 kilometers) per hour in a circle. The huge storm moves forward over the water. When the hurricane gets to land, the winds slow down. Hurricanes can last for a week or longer.

Tornadoes are storms that develop over land. Winds whirl around the center of the storm. Winds can blow more than 200 miles (322 kilometers) per hour. They can happen throughout the world. In the U.S. the tornado season is during spring and early summer. Tornadoes usually last between a minute and an hour.

Read the following list of facts. For each fact, write H on the line if it is true for hurricanes only, T on the line if it is true for tornadoes only, and B on the line if it is true for both kinds of storms.

_____ 1. This storm develops over the ocean.

_____ 2. This storm carries winds of more than 200 miles per hour.

_____ 3. This storm develops over the land.

_____ 4. This storm occurs most often in spring and early summer.

_____ 5. This storm has winds of more than 75 miles per hour.

_____ 6. This storm can develop in the United States.

_____ 7. This storm could occur in the month of June.

_____ 8. This storm can last for a whole week.

_____ 9. This storm is often over within minutes.

Name _____

Nature Walk Collections

Look at Ken's and Maria's collections. Answer the questions that follow.

1. Which student has collected something that was a home for a bird?

   _____

2. Which student seems more interested in leaves? _____

3. What three things did Maria find that Ken does not have? _____

   _____

4. What three things did Ken find that Maria does not have? _____

   _____

5. What four things did they both find? _____

   _____

6. Whose collection contains all things that come from a tree? _____

7. Who collected something that can grow in the dark? _____

   What is it? _____

Name _____

 Elephants

Read about the two kinds of elephants. Compare the elephants by filling in the information below. If the information was not given in the article, fill in the blank with "not given."

• •

There are two kinds of elephants living today, the Indian elephant and the African elephant. The Indian elephant is smaller, stands about ten feet (3 meters) tall, and weighs about 4 tons (3.6 metric tons). It has smaller ears, a high forehead, and only one lip at the end of its smooth trunk. There are five nails on each of its front feet and four on each hind foot. Only the male has tusks, which are small. The Indian elephant is usually the one seen in zoos.

The African elephant is around 11 feet (3.3 meters) tall and weighs about 6 tons (5.4 metric tons). Its ears are big, and its forehead is sloped. Its front feet each have four nails, and the hind feet each have three nails. Also, its trunk is ringed, and its tusks are large.

	Indian Elephants	African Elephants
Height:	a. _____	b. _____
Weight:	c. _____	d. _____
Ears:	e. _____	f. _____
Forehead:	g. _____	h. _____
Lips:	i. _____	j. _____
Skin on trunk:	k. _____	l. _____
Tusks:	m. _____	n. _____
Nails:	o. _____	p. _____

Ping and Pong

Both Ping and Pong are from outer space. Read their stories. Answer the questions.

· ·

Ping is from the planet Green. He sleeps all day long, nibbling on his fingernails, which are carrots. Ping gets up at the crack of dusk to go to work. He repairs flying saucers at the Drag In–Fly Out Repair Shop.

Pong is from the planet Red. He has to be careful not to squish his toes, which are grapes. Pong sleeps at night but gets up early to pilot the Flying Saucer Emergency Repair transport.

1. What is similar about the names of Ping's and Pong's planets? _____

    _____

2. Which alien would be better at fixing a flying saucer? _____

3. Which alien would be better at flying a flying saucer? _____

4. Which alien uses his fingernails for snacks? _____

5. Which alien sleeps at night? _____

6. Which alien sleeps all day? _____

7. What kind of job could Ping do best on Earth? _____

    _____

8. Circle the best Earth job for Pong:

    ambulance driver   car mechanic

Name _____

Josh and the Eyes at the Door

Read the two stories. Complete the chart by putting an **X** in the box if the information applies to either Josh or Dominic or both.

Josh heard something outside in the woods. Josh lit the candle by his bed. There was no window in the little cabin. Josh got up and looked out the front door. Little dark eyes, which were part of a great big dark face, looked back at him.

Slam! Josh shut the door. He put the big wood bar across it. He ran over to the bed and shook his father. "Pa," he said. "There is a bear outside but I have locked the door!"

Dominic heard something outside. He turned on his flashlight and looked out his window. Little dark eyes looked up at him. The little dark eyes were part of a great big dark face.

Oh, my! Josh ran to his parent's room and shook his father. "Dad," he said. " There is a bear in the back yard."

	Josh	Dominic
door		
father		
outside		
dark eyes		
candle		
window		
bear		
flashlight		

Poodle School

Princess, Percival, and Pru all go to the same school. Compare their Monday schedules. Answer the questions.

Princess		Percival		Pru	
8:00	Barking	8:00	Napping	8:00	Looking Cute
9:00	Chasing Cats	9:00	Shaking Hands	9:00	Howling
10:00	Howling	10:00	Begging	10:00	Barking
11:00	Looking Cute	11:00	Howling	11:00	Chasing Cats
12:00	Lunch	12:00	Lunch	12:00	Lunch
1:00	Napping	1:00	Barking	1:00	Begging
2:00	Begging	2:00	Chasing Cats	2:00	Napping
3:00	Go Home	3:00	Go Home	3:00	Go Home

1. Which two poodles have barking class before lunch?

    _____

2. Which poodle chases cats in the afternoon?

    _____

3. Which poodle is the only one to practice shaking hands on Mondays?

    _____

4. Which poodle has begging in the morning?

    _____

5. Which two poodles practice napping after lunch?

    _____

6. Which subject do all three poodles study before lunch?

    _____

7. When Princess and the class finish their looking-cute practice, where do they go next?

    _____

Mollusks

Read the passage and complete the activity on the next page.

••

Mollusks are animals with no backbone. Their soft bodies are usually covered by hard shells. On many beaches you will find the shells. We call them seashells. Most of the shells you find on the beach are empty.

The mollusks family is divided into seven classes. Only some of them have hard shells. Gastropoda is one class of mollusks. Most gastropods have a single, coiled shell. Included in this class are limpets, slugs, and snails. They can be found in the Atlantic and Pacific Oceans in North America.

Bivalves make up another large class of mollusks. The shells of bivalves are two shells hinged together. The animals that call these shells home include clams, oysters, mussels, and scallops. They, too, are found on both coasts of North America.

A third class of mollusks are chitons. Their bodies are covered by eight shell plates. The plates look something like a turtle's shell. Chitons and mossy mopalia are all included in this class. Chitons live in shallow rock pools. They live along the Pacific Ocean from Alaska to Mexico.

Compare and Contrast • CD-104540

Name _____

Use the facts from the passage to answer the questions.

• •

	gastropods	bivalves	chitons
1. What do their shells look like?	a.	b.	c.
2. Where can they be found?	d.	e.	f.
3. List mollusks included in each group.	g.	h.	i.

What Is a Platypus?

You may never see a platypus. But as you read about the animal you can picture it in your mind by comparing it with other animals. Underline the ways a platypus is like a duck in **red**. Underline the ways a platypus is like a beaver in **blue**. (Hint: Remember a beaver is a mammal and a duck is a bird.) Use the passage to draw the missing body parts on the drawing below.

• •

A platypus looks like a mix of a beaver and a duck. The male platypus has stingers like bees. The stingers are in its rear feet and are used for protection. At first, scientists did not believe the platypus was real. They thought someone was trying to trick them.

A platypus hunts underwater, paddling with its web feet like a duck. A strong flat tail steers it. The tail of a platypus looks much like a beaver's tail. A rubbery bill scoops up insects and shellfish from among the mud at the bottom. Mud and gravel come mixed with the food. Like a bird, a platypus does not have teeth. So the gravel helps "grind" up the food.

Platypuses build nests on or near the water. Unlike most other mammals the platypus lays eggs. The female keeps the eggs warm with her velvety fur while they hatch. She then feeds the young milk like other mammals.

What Is a Platypus? (cont.)

Compare the facts about the platypus on the left to the list of animals on the right. In each space write the letter of the word or phrase that completes the sentence.

· ·

1. The platypus lays eggs like _____ .

2. The platypus has a bill and webbed feet like _____ .

3. The platypus swims with a long, flat tail like _____ .

4. The platypus uses a stinger for protection like _____ .

5. The platypus has no teeth like ____ .

6. The platypus builds a nest on the ground near the water like _____ .

7. The female platypus produces milk for its young like _____ .

a. a duck

b. a beaver

c. neither the duck and the beaver

d. both the duck and the beaver

27

Whale or Fish?

Chu wanted to know whether Moby, a sea creature at the aquarium, is a whale or just a large fish. Fill in the chart at the bottom of the page. On the next page you will use these facts to help answer Chu's question about the sea creature.

• •

Whales live in salt water. They are huge animals with smooth, rubbery skin. Their tails swing up and down while swimming. Even though they live in the water, whales breathe oxygen and have lungs. Instead of breathing through a nose, whales breathe through a blowhole. People locate a whale by seeing the spray from the blowhole. The females give birth to one baby at a time. Baby whales are fed milk like other mammals. Whales are warm-blooded. Their body temperature never changes. A thick layer of fat keeps the temperature of the whale's body consistent. This layer of fat is called **blubber**.

Fish are found in salt and in fresh water. Fish come in all sizes. Sharks are the biggest fish. The biggest shark was about 65 feet (20 meters) long. Most are much smaller than whales. A fish's body is covered with bony scales. Fish have tail fins that are straight up and down. Fish swim by moving their tail fins from side to side. Fish have gills that are able to take oxygen out of the water. To stay alive the fish need the water. Fish are cold-blooded; their body temperature changes with the temperature of the water. Most fish lay eggs in the water. After a time the eggs hatch. Most parent fish do care for the eggs or the young.

	Whales	**Fish**
type of water		
skin		
tail moves		
breathing		
body temperature		

Name _____

Compare the **Moby Facts** to the whale and fish facts on the last page. Put an **X** in front of the facts listed below that could help Chu identify to which group Moby belonged.

• •

Moby Facts

_____ 1. This type of animal may measure over 67 feet (20 meters) long.

_____ 2. Their brains are the largest of any animal.

_____ 3. Spray from blowhole can be seen from far away.

_____ 4. The creature's teeth are over eight inches (20 centimeters) long.

_____ 5. It devours giant squid, other whales, and fish.

_____ 6. A famous story tells of how the creature damaged and sank whaling ships with one downward slap of its huge tail.

_____ 7. During the 18th century these creatures were hunted for a waxy material their bodies produced. The wax, along with blubber, was used in making candles and soaps.

_____ 8. Blubber helps the animal's body temperature stay the same, even in cold water.

Try This: On another sheet of paper draw a picture of Moby.

Name _____

Read the postcards Amy received over summer vacation. Contrast her friends' vacations by filling in the chart.

• •

Dear Amy,
    We are having so much fun here! We are staying in a cool hotel with a swimming pool and a mini-golf course! We have been going to the beach every day too. I can't wait to show you the shells I found! We went out for a seafood dinner last night. See you when I get back.
        JoAnn

Dear Amy,
    I can't believe how awful this week is going. It has rained every day, and I came down with a cold. We are staying with my aunt. It is so boring! We did go shopping one day and I got a new book.
    See you soon (I hope!),
        Maria

	JoAnn	**Maria**
Where is each girl staying?	a.	b.
How does each girl feel about her trip?	c.	d.
List one thing each girl did while she was gone.	e.	f.
Describe the souvenir each girl is bringing home.	g.	h.

Analogies

Analogies make a statement by comparing two things. Use what you know about that pair of words to complete the second comparison. The second comparison should show the same relationship as the first one. Example: Beef is to meat as apple is to fruit.

• •

Word Bank

quietly	hot	100	bird	read
clock	water	eight	pounds	

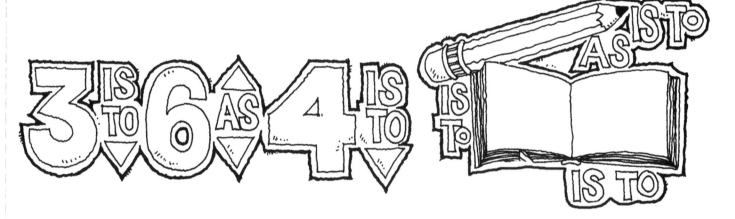

1. Three is to six as four is to _____.

2. Whale is to mammal as eagle is to _____.

3. Length is to inches as weight is to _____.

4. Loud is to loudly as quiet is to _____.

5. Date is to calendar as time is to _____.

6. Cool is to cold as warm is to _____.

7. 25 is to 50 as 50 is to _____.

8. Pencil is to write as book is to _____.

9. Airplane is to sky as boat is to _____.

Name _____

Kids Count!

Read the newspaper article about the two student volunteers. Answer the questions.

• •

Student Volunteers Make a Difference

GREENE, MA- Annabelle Davis and Antonio Grillo both volunteer for our town. Here is how these two students help:

Each spring Annabelle volunteers. She works with her mother. She helps to raise funds for a community garden. In the summer, Annabelle volunteers 10 hours a week. She works at the garden. She helps older gardeners weed. She waters their garden. She also looks after younger children. That gives their parents time to work in their gardens.

Annabelle and Antonio

Antonio visits retirement homes. These homes are in the Greene area. He makes two visits a month. He spends time talking with the people who live in the homes. He also plays the piano and puts on magic shows. Everyone looks forward to Antonio's lively visits. He makes these visits with his father.

1. Where does Annabelle do her volunteer work? _____

   _____

2. Where does Antonio do his volunteer work? _____

3. Who does volunteer work all year long? _____

4. Who does volunteer work mostly in the summer? _____

5. Whose volunteer work is done outdoors? _____

6. If Annabelle looked for a new volunteer job, which one do you think she would pick?

   hospital assistant   nature center guide

7. If Antonio had time to teach other students, which subject do you think he would pick?

   swimming   piano   karate

More Analogies

Circle the word that belongs on each line.

• •

1. Companion is to friend as winner is to _____.

    loser   champion   knight

2. Guess is to suppose as certain is to _____.

    positive   accident   discourage

3. Accept is to deny as brave is to _____.

    reward   fierce   cowardly

4. Decrease is to lessen as maintain is to _____.

    remain   increase   reduce

5. Summer is to season as inch is to _____.

    year   measurement   hour

6. Pint is to quart as foot is to _____.

    hour   gallon   yard

7. True is to false as typical is to _____.

    rare   usual   common

8. Grasp is to hold as fearful is to _____.

    relaxed   frightened   joyful

9. Depend is to dependable as reach is to _____.

    reaching   reached   reachable

Try this: How is grasp related to hold? On a separate piece of paper write three other word pairs that are related in the same way.

33

Pen Pals

The following are letters that Terry received from two of his friends who had gone away over spring vacation. Read the two letters. Answer the questions that follow.

• •

Dear Terry,

    Hi from New York City. So far I have been to two museums. The Metropolitan Museum of Art was great. The American Museum of Natural History took all day. The art museum had over two million works of art! We saw dinosaur bones at the Natural History Museum. We also took a tour of the NBC studios at Rockefeller Center. For lunch we went to Central Park. Monday we are going to take the ferry to see the Statue of Liberty. Then we visit the Empire State Building.

                Charles

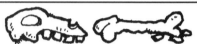

Dear Terry,

    We are having a great time in Los Angeles! Yesterday we went to the Natural History Museum. We saw bones from prehistoric animals. It was so cool! We've also been to Griffith Park. There we visited a butterfly garden. Yesterday, we took a tour of the NBC studios. Tuesday, we are going to Anaheim. That is where Disneyland is! I can't wait! See you in a few days.

           Your Buddy,
           Aaron

1.   Which city has the Empire State Building? _____

2.   Which city has a butterfly garden inside a park? _____

3.   Which friend saw dinosaur bones in a museum? _____

4.   Which friend visited a museum with many paintings? _____

5.   What tour were both friends able to take on their different trips? _____

_____

6.   In what city is Disneyland? _____

7.   In what city is Central Park? _____

Name _____

Read each sentence. If it tells how the Earth is the same as the moon, write **same**. If it tells how it is different, write **different**.

• •

1. There are oceans on Earth, but there is no water on the moon.

    _____

2. People live on Earth, but nobody lives on the moon. _____

3. The Earth is shaped like a ball, and so is the moon. _____

4. The gravity of the Earth pulls on the moon, and the gravity of the moon pulls on the Earth. _____

5. There are many plants and animals on the Earth, but there are none on the moon. _____

6. A day lasts about twelve hours on the Earth, but it lasts about a month on the moon. _____

Now or Then?

Read the passage on this page. Complete the activity on the next page.

• •

Have you ridden in a convertible car? A convertible can have the top of the car up or down. Riding in a convertible can be fun. Long ago when Henry Ford started making cars, most cars were convertibles. Ford made the cars very cheap. That way more people were able to afford them. The cars could not go as fast as the cars we drive today, but they looked like a lot of fun!

Ford's cars were different from the cars that you see today. The cars did use gas, but the tank was under the driver's seat, so people had to lift the seat out to put gas in the car. Sometimes the cars would not start in cold weather unless people poured hot water on the motor. Many of the cars did not have bumpers or mirrors. Those things cost extra money. Still, the cars were a great way to get around, just as our cars are today.

Name _____

Would you rather have a car from the past or a car from today? Make a list of how cars today are the same as cars of the past . Next make a list of the differences to help you decide.

• •

How Cars of the Past and Cars of Today Are Alike:

1. _____

_____

2. _____

_____

3. _____

_____

How Cars of the Past and Cars of Today Are Different:

1. _____

_____

2. _____

_____

3. _____

_____

Sara's Sweet Green Grass

Read the following story. Complete the activities on the next page.

• •

The first pink of the Mojave Desert dawn showed at the opening of Sara's burrow. She was hungry. It was time to go out and find some fresh grass to eat. Maybe there would even be a few wild poppies left.

Many other animals were out enjoying the cool March morning. A hummingbird whizzed by on his way to the flower fields down the hill. A cottontail bunny stopped to look at Sara. His nose twitched. Then he hopped away.

Sara wondered what it would be like to fly like the hummingbird or hop like the rabbit. Then she saw some sweet green grass. It was in the shade of a big Joshua tree.

The grass was not close, but it was not that far away. If Sara kept going she would have plenty of time. She could eat and get back to her burrow before the sun got too hot.

A pack rat dashed past Sara. His cheeks were full of food. Sara put one foot in front of the other. She stopped and rested when she got tired. She crossed the place where a small stream had run when it rained in January. The water had been sweet. She remembered the long drinks she had taken. It had been worth waking up from her winter sleep.

Sara climbed over a rock carefully. Having a shell was good protection, but if she ended up on her back, it would be hard to turn over again. The grass was close now. She took her first bite. She did not care if she could not fly or hop or run. She had eaten green grass every spring for sixty years and it was always good.

Name _____

Sara's Sweet Grass (cont.)

A girl named Katy lives in a desert town not far from Sara's home. In some ways, Katy's life is like Sara's. In other ways, their lives are very different. Read each pair of sentences. If they tell how Sara's life is the same as Katy's, circle the word **same**. If they tell how Sara's life is different from Katy's, circle **different**.

• •

1. Sara is a desert tortoise. Katy is a girl.   same   different

2. Sara lives in a burrow. Katy lives in a house.   same   different

3. Sara eats in the morning. Katy does too.   same   different

4. Sara can live more than 60 years. Katy can too.   same   different

5. Sara does not have wings. Katy does not either.   same   different

6. Sara can go for years without drinking water.
   Katy needs water every day.   same   different

7. Sara sleeps all winter. Katy does not.   same   different

8. Sara has four legs. Katy has two.   same   different

Try this: On a separate piece of paper write more ways
Sara and Katy are the same.

Special Days

Read the following passage. Complete the activity on the next page.

• •

July 4 is an American holiday. It is Independence Day. On July 4, 1776, America became a new country. It was no longer a part of England. On this day people celebrate freedom. There are parades. Many people watch fireworks. Flags are flown. **Independence** means to take care of yourself. That is how the day got its name.

Canada also has an Independence Day. Canada became free from France on July 1, 1867. Canada became a new country. In Canada this day is also called Canada Day. Fireworks and concerts are enjoyed on this day. July 1 is a day of firsts in Canada. It is a day of new things. The first radio network opened July 1, 1927. The first TV show was seen across Canada on July 1, 1958.

Name _____

Use the passage to answer the questions. Circle the correct answer.

• •

1. What is being compared in the story?

    A. freedom in America

    B. Independence Day in America and Canada

    C. radio and television in America and Canada

2. What is the same in both America and Canada?

    A. Both countries celebrate on the same day.

    B. Both countries became free from France.

    C. Both celebrate with fireworks.

3. What are three ways people celebrate Independence Day in America?

    _____

    _____

    _____

4. What are two ways people celebrate Independence Day in Canada?

    _____

    _____

5. What is one way both countries celebrate Independence Day?

    _____

Name _____

Two Islands

Life on the Hawaii and the Solomon Islands is similar and yet very different. Which one would you like to call home? Study the chart of facts below. In each row put a big ✓ in the square with the condition you would chose for your island home. At the end of the chart write the name of your favorite island. Complete the activity on the next page.

	Hawaii	Solomon Islands
Major Islands	8 islands in the middle of the Pacific Ocean (an area of 6,423 square miles or 10220 square kilometers)	5 larger islands and over 900 smaller islands and reefs, not far from Australia (a total area of 11,599 square miles or 18666 square kilometers)
Population In 2010	1,360,301 people living there (with an average of 211 people per square mile, much like a city)	510,000 people living there (with an average only 19 people per square mile, more rural lifestyle)
Languages Spoken	English is the official and most often spoken language.	English is the official language, but over 63 other languages are spoken on the islands.
Crops Grown/ Products Made	Pineapple, sugar, flowers, and macadamia nuts are the major crops grown on the islands.	Wood products, palm tree oil, bananas, chocolate, and pineapple are the major products and crops of the islands.
Largest Industry, Type of Work Done by Residents	tourist trade, coffee, sugar, and pineapple About one out of three people work serving tourists. Most Hawaiians live and work in the largest city.	farming and fishing Three out of four people work or live on farms and in small towns. One in four people cannot read. Children are not required to attend school.
Favorite Sports	surfing, swimming, boating, hiking, fishing	soccer, rugby, cricket, observing nature while diving and snorkeling
Climate and Weather	Tropical: warm, gentle winds, sunny skies all year, some rain Oct. to March	Tropical: very warm with a lot of rain every month of the year, frequent winds
My Favorite Island Is		

Two Islands

Complete the following.

• •

1. Write two sentences explaining how you chose your favorite island on the last page. Your statements should include three things that you compared in making your choice.

_____

_____

_____

_____

2. Write two sentences comparing and contrasting the weather and climate of the two islands. In your sentences make sure you explain how the weather on the two islands is similar and how it is different.

_____

_____

_____

_____

Happy New Year!

Read the story and answer the questions on the next page.

• •

Jean's family lives in France. On New Year's Eve they have a huge supper. Jean gets to stay up late. At midnight they kiss under the mistletoe. They also exchange holiday gifts.

Hua's family lives in China. On the Chinese New Year, the whole family has a big feast. Hua and the other children get "lucky money." The "money" is in red envelopes from their parents. Then Hua and her family go out to a festival. Lines of dancers dance in the street in costumes. People set off firecrackers to welcome the new year.

Gary's family lives in the U.S. On New Year's Eve, they host a party for family and friends. They have a big meal together. Then they pop popcorn. Gary gets to stay up until midnight. Then everybody throws confetti, blows noisemakers, and kisses each other.

Name _____

Use the information from the story to answer the questions. Put a **T** on the line before the statement if it is true, and an **F** on the line before the statement if it is false.

• •

_____ 1. All the celebrations include a large meal.

_____ 2. Jean's celebration includes firecrackers.

_____ 3. Jean and Gary get to stay up late on New Year's Eve.

_____ 4. Hua receives "lucky money" in red envelopes.

_____ 5. Gary's family exchanges gifts as part of their celebration.

_____ 6. Jean gets to see people dance in costumes at a festival.

_____ 7. Hua's and Jean's families kiss at midnight.

_____ 8. Gary's family throws confetti at midnight.

Answer Key

Page 4
1. a; 2. b; 3. b; 4. a; 5. b; 6. a; 7. b

Page 5
1. ball; 2. George; 3. Princess;
4. George; 5. Princess; Answers will vary; possible answers include: Dog has key, has other dogs over for tea.

Page 6
1. Tuesday; 2. Wednesday; 3. no;
4. Thursday; 5. Tuesday; 6. Monday

Page 7
1. a. NF; b. F; 2. a. F; b. NF; 3. a. NF; b. F; 4. a. NF; b. F; 5. a. F; b. NF; 6. a. NF; b. F; 7. a. F; b. NF

Page 8
Circle: 1. letter; 2. strong; 3. trail; 4. cow; 5. swift; 6. crib; 7. wood;
8. sparrow; 9. brother

Page 9
1. animals with spots; 2. big cats;
3. Answers will vary. possible answer: Animal Venn Diagram; 4. Circle 1: Answers will vary. possible answer: Animals with spots; Circle 2: Answers will vary. possible answer: big cats

Page 10
Underline in Blue: floating ice, very cold, floats on Artic Ocean, first reached by Peary who used dogsleds, the USS Nautilus traveled under the pole. Underline in Red: land covered by ice and snow, on continent of Antarctica, coldest and driest place on Earth, blanket of ice over two miles thick, first reached by Amundsen using dogsleds

Page 11
Answers will vary using the following in any order: North Pole: is ice not land, floats on Artic, discovered by Peary, Nautilus traveled under it; South Pole: land, covered by ice and snow, continent of Antarctica, coldest and driest place on earth, discovered by Amundsen; Both: magnetic poles, ice and snow, very cold, dogsleds used by explorers.

Page 12
1. Daniel; 2. Jan; 3. Kurt; 4. Kurt;
5. Daniel; 6. Kurt; 7. Kurt and Daniel;
8. Kurt and Daniel

Page 13
Clothing: dress, hat, shirt, shoes; School Workers: secretary, principal, bus driver, teacher; Toys: doll, ball, skateboard, train; Things to Read: book, newspaper, letter, magazine; Writing Tools: crayon, pen, pencil, marker; Kitchen Tools: bowl, pan, spoon, knife

Page 14

1. f; 2. c; 3. a; 4. e; 5. b; 6. d;
7. popsicle/ice; 8. dough/clay;
9. clown/hyena

Page 15

1. Yes; 2. No; 3. No; 4. Yes; 5. No;
6. Jeff; 7. Derek; 8. Derek; 9. Jeff

Pages 16–17

Football: played in United States,
played in Canada, uses oval ball,
field is 120 yards by 54 yards, player
runs or passes ball, touchdown is 6
points; Soccer: played all over the
world, field is 100–130 yards by 50–
100 yards, player kicks or heads ball,
goal is 1 point; Both: played on field,
2 teams with 11 players, players wear
protective equipment

Page 18

1. H; 2. T; 3. T; 4. T; 5. H; 6. B; 7. B; 8. H;
9. T

Page 19

1. Ken; 2. Maria; 3. lilac leaves, maple
leaf, stick; 4. nest, mushroom, maple
seed; 5. pine needles, poplar leaf,
acorn, pine cone; 6. Maria; 7. Ken,
mushroom

Page 20

a. 10 feet; b. 11 feet; c. 4 tons;
d. 6 tons; e. small; f. big; g. high;
h. sloped; i. one; j. not given;
k. smooth; l. ringed; m. male-small;
n. large; o. 5 on front feet, 4 on hind
feet; p. 4 on front feet, 3 on hind feet

Page 21

1. named after colors; 2. Ping;
3. Pong; 4. Ping; 5. Pong; 6. Ping;
7. Answer will vary. possible answer:
auto mechanic; 8. ambulance driver

Page 22

Josh: door, bear, candle, father,
outside, dark eyes; Dominic: window,
bear, father, outside, dark eyes,
flashlight

Page 23

1. Princess, Pru; 2. Percival; 3. Percival;
4. Percival; 5. Princess, Pru; 6. howling;
7. lunch

Pages 24–25

a. single, coiled; b. 2 shells, hinged
together; c. eight shell plates; d.
North America; e. North America;
f. Pacific Ocean; g. limpets, slugs,
snails; h. clams, oysters, mussels,
scallops; i. chitons, mossy mopalia

Page 26

Underline Red: rubbery bill, web feet,
no teeth, nests, lay eggs, hatch eggs;
Underline Blue: females produce
milk, tail

Page 27

1. a; 2. a; 3. b; 4. c; 5. a; 6. d; 7. b

Page 28

Whales: salt; smooth, rubbery; up
and down; blowhole; warm blooded;
Fish: fresh or salt; hard scales; side to
side; gills; cold blooded

Page 29
X marked: 3, 6, 8

Page 30
a. hotel; b. with aunt; c. having fun;
d. bored and ill; e. Possible answer:
went to beach; f. Possible answer:
went shopping; g. shells; h. new book

Page 31
1. eight; 2. bird; 3. pounds; 4. quietly;
5. clock; 6. hot; 7. 100; 8. read;
9. water

Page 32
1. community garden; 2. retirement
homes; 3. Antonio; 4. Annabelle;
5. Annabelle; 6. nature center guide;
7. piano

Page 33
1. champion; 2. positive; 3. cowardly;
4. remain; 5. measurement; 6. yard;
7. rare; 8. frightened; 9. reachable

Page 34
1. New York City; 2. Los Angeles;
3. both; 4. Charles; 5. NBC studios;
6. Anaheim; 7. New York City

Page 35
1. different; 2. different; 3. same;
4. same; 5. different; 6. different

Pages 36–37
Alike: Possible answers: both use
gas, great way to get around, both
available as convertibles; Different:
old cars did not go very fast, gas tank
under front seat in old cars, some old
cars did not have bumpers or mirrors

Pages 38–39
1. different; 2. different; 3. same; 4.
same; 5. same; 6. different;
7. different; 8. different

Pages 40–41
1. b; 2. c; 3. fireworks, flags, parades;
4. fireworks, concerts; 5. fireworks

Page 42
Check one item in each row. Answers
will vary but should be either Hawaii
or Solomon Islands

Page 43
1. Answers will vary but should
include three comparisons in
sentence form. 2. Answers will vary
but should include comparisons
or contrasts regarding climate or
weather in sentence form.

Pages 44–45
1. T; 2. F; 3, T; 4. T; 5. F; 6. F; 7. F; 8. T

Compare and Contrast • CD-104540